Dream Interpretation: A Journey Through the Mind's Mirror

Catherine J Rosser

Published by Catherine J Rosser, 2024.

DREAM INTERPRETATION: A JOURNEY THROUGH THE MIND'S MIRROR

First edition. October 25, 2024.

Copyright © 2024 Catherine J Rosser.

ISBN: 979-8227093394

Written by Catherine J Rosser.

Table of Contents

Chapter 1: Introduction to Dream Interpretation

What Are Dreams?

Dreams are a natural phenomenon that occur during sleep, when the mind enters various stages of rest, particularly Rapid Eye Movement (REM) sleep. During this stage, the brain is active, producing vivid images, emotions, and narratives. These dream experiences often feel lifelike, yet they can defy the laws of time, space, and logic.

Dreams have long been considered a window into the unconscious mind, revealing hidden truths about our emotions, desires, fears, and unresolved conflicts. Though the exact purpose of dreams remains a mystery, modern science suggests they may serve multiple functions, such as consolidating memories, processing emotions, and problem-solving.

A Brief History of Dream Interpretation

Dream interpretation dates back thousands of years, with evidence from ancient Egypt, Mesopotamia, Greece, and China. Dreams were often seen as divine messages or omens, revealing truths about the future or providing insight into the dreamer's life. For instance, the ancient Egyptians viewed dreams as a form of communication with gods, while ancient Greeks believed dreams could offer healing and guidance.

In modern history, dream interpretation gained scientific credibility with the emergence of psychoanalysis. Sigmund

Freud and Carl Jung, two pioneers of dream analysis, offered distinct yet complementary views on dreams.

Freud: Believed dreams were a manifestation of repressed desires, particularly sexual or aggressive impulses. He developed the concepts of manifest content (the literal dream narrative) and latent content (the hidden psychological meaning).

Jung: Expanded on Freud's ideas, suggesting that dreams were not only personal but also connected to the collective unconscious. Jung introduced the idea of archetypes—universal symbols and themes present in dreams across all cultures.

Modern Psychological Theories

Activation-Synthesis Theory: Proposed by Hobson and McCarley, this theory suggests that dreams are a result of the brain attempting to make sense of random neural activity during sleep. According to this theory, dreams are the brain's attempt to create a coherent story from chaotic stimuli.

Problem-Solving Theory: This theory, supported by cognitive scientists, posits that dreams help us solve real-life problems by allowing us to process complex situations and emotions in a low-stakes environment.

Emotional Processing: Psychologists believe dreams allow us to process emotions in a safe and unconscious manner, enabling us to work through difficult experiences, trauma, or stress.

Why Understanding Dreams Is Important

Interpreting dreams can offer profound insight into the dreamer's psychological state, unresolved conflicts, and inner desires. Understanding dreams can also foster creativity, provide emotional release, and aid in personal development. By exploring the symbolic nature of dreams, individuals can uncover deeper truths about their lives and well-being.

Chapter 2: Types of Dreams

Lucid Dreams

Lucid dreams occur when the dreamer becomes aware that they are dreaming, often leading to the ability to control or influence the dream narrative. Lucid dreamers can consciously explore their dreams, create desired scenarios, or confront fears in a safe, imagined environment. Techniques for inducing lucid dreams, such as reality checks or mnemonic induction, are covered in this section.

Lucid dreams have become popular not only for personal exploration but also for therapeutic purposes. Studies suggest they can be used to address recurring nightmares, increase creativity, and promote self-awareness.

Nightmares

Nightmares are dreams that provoke intense fear, anxiety, or distress. They often involve themes of danger, threats, or personal loss, and can sometimes result from traumatic experiences or high stress levels. Nightmares are a reflection of the subconscious mind's attempt to process unresolved fear or anxiety.

Understanding the root causes of nightmares can be therapeutic. This section offers techniques for addressing recurring nightmares, including dream rehearsal therapy, cognitive-behavioral therapy (CBT), and relaxation techniques.

Recurring Dreams

4

Recurring dreams feature repeated scenarios, themes, or symbols over time. These dreams often indicate unresolved issues or emotions that have yet to be addressed. Recurring dreams can persist for months, years, or even a lifetime.

The key to unlocking recurring dreams is to analyze their symbolic content, emotional undertones, and the specific situations that trigger them in waking life. This section provides case studies of recurring dreams and practical advice for breaking their cycle by confronting the root emotional cause.

Daydreams

Daydreams, unlike nighttime dreams, occur while we are awake. They allow the mind to drift into a semi-conscious state, often bringing fantasies, desires, or creative solutions to the forefront. While often dismissed as unproductive, daydreams can serve as a form of problem-solving and creative thinking.

This section explores how daydreams differ from nighttime dreams and how intentional daydreaming can lead to breakthroughs in personal and professional life.

Prophetic Dreams

Prophetic dreams have been reported across cultures and time periods, where dreamers claim to have seen events in their dreams that later occurred in waking life. While scientifically difficult to validate, many individuals believe prophetic dreams reveal future events or offer warnings.

This section examines historical accounts of prophetic dreams, their cultural significance, and possible psychological explanations, including heightened awareness and subconscious pattern recognition.

Healing Dreams

Healing dreams are thought to promote physical, emotional, or spiritual healing. Dreamers may receive guidance on personal well-being, unresolved emotional wounds, or unresolved conflicts.

In some cases, these dreams may involve symbols of rebirth, transformation, or the appearance of a guiding figure, such as a healer or spiritual entity. The section includes stories of dreamers who have experienced profound healing as a result of their dreams.

Chapter 3: Common Dream Symbols and Their Meanings

Natural Elements

Water: Water is one of the most common symbols in dreams and is often associated with emotions and the unconscious mind. Calm water may suggest emotional tranquility, while turbulent water could indicate emotional upheaval or repressed feelings.

Fire: Fire often symbolizes transformation, passion, or destruction. Being burned by fire may represent feelings of anger or the desire for purification. Fire can also indicate a major life change or a burning desire to achieve a goal.

Earth: Earth typically represents grounding, stability, or nurturing. Being buried in the earth may suggest feelings of being overwhelmed or trapped, while walking on fertile soil might symbolize growth and personal development.

Wind: Wind often symbolizes change, intellect, or freedom. A strong gust of wind may represent mental or emotional turmoil, while a gentle breeze can suggest spiritual awakening or a change of mindset.

Animals

Snakes: Snakes can represent transformation, healing, or hidden fears. In some cultures, they symbolize wisdom, while in others they are seen as deceptive. The context of the snake in the dream—whether it is threatening or benevolent—can significantly alter its meaning.

Birds: Birds are commonly associated with freedom, aspirations, and the soul. A flying bird may represent a desire to break free from limitations, while a caged bird might symbolize a feeling of being trapped or constrained.

Cats: Cats can represent independence, mystery, or intuition. A playful cat might symbolize creativity and curiosity, while an aggressive cat could indicate repressed emotions or a need for self-defense.

Wolves: Wolves often represent instincts, power, and primal urges. A lone wolf may signify independence and self-reliance, while a pack of wolves might suggest a need for community or confrontation with a group dynamic.

Human Body Parts

Eyes: The eyes are often symbolic of insight, awareness, or perception. Seeing clearly through your eyes in a dream may represent clarity of thought, while blurred vision might suggest confusion or avoidance of a truth.

Teeth: Dreams of teeth falling out are common and are usually associated with feelings of insecurity or loss. They may represent concerns about one's appearance, fear of aging, or anxiety about communication.

Hands: Hands are powerful symbols of action, creation, and connection. Losing the use of your hands may suggest feelings of helplessness, while strong hands may symbolize empowerment and control.

Hair: Hair often symbolizes strength, beauty, and identity. Cutting or losing hair in a dream may suggest feelings of vulnerability or loss of power.

Emotions in Dreams

Fear: Fear in dreams often represents unresolved anxieties or the anticipation of change. Facing fearful situations in a dream can provide insight into your waking concerns and offer an opportunity for self-reflection.

Joy: Feelings of joy in dreams may reflect contentment, success, or fulfillment in your waking life. Dream joy often signals alignment with your values and desires.

Anger: Dreams involving anger may suggest repressed frustrations or unresolved conflict in your life. Understanding the root of this anger can provide clues to emotional healing.

Sadness: Sadness in dreams may indicate a need to process grief, loss, or disappointment. It can also represent feelings of isolation or a need for emotional release.

Objects

Keys: Keys are often symbolic of access, opportunity, or hidden knowledge. Finding a key may represent discovering a new solution, while losing a key might signify missed opportunities or feelings of inadequacy.

Clocks: Clocks often represent time, deadlines, or the passage of life. A ticking clock may suggest pressure or a sense of urgency, while a broken clock could indicate feelings of being out of control or frozen in time.

Mirrors: Mirrors in dreams symbolize self-reflection, truth, and identity. Looking into a mirror may suggest a need to examine one's true self, while a distorted reflection might represent confusion about identity or self-perception.

Money: Money in dreams can symbolize self-worth, power, and resources. Gaining money may represent success and abundance, while losing money could indicate feelings of insecurity or fear of financial loss.

Chapter 4: Dream Settings

Dream settings often reflect the dreamer's mental and emotional state, as well as their perception of life circumstances. The environments in which dreams unfold can provide clues to the underlying meaning of the dream. In this chapter, we explore common dream settings and their symbolic interpretations.

Houses and Buildings

Houses often represent the self or different aspects of the dreamer's life, with different rooms symbolizing different parts of the psyche or life experience. For instance, the basement may represent the subconscious mind or repressed memories, while the attic can symbolize higher thoughts, wisdom, or forgotten memories.

New House: A new house may suggest new opportunities, personal growth, or changes in identity.

Old or Dilapidated House: This could represent neglected areas of the dreamer's life or outdated beliefs and feelings.

School or Office Buildings: Often represent learning experiences, work stress, or feelings of inadequacy in professional life.

Schools

Schools are common dream settings that usually symbolize learning, personal growth, or unresolved issues from childhood or adolescence. Dreams about being in school might suggest that the dreamer is learning lessons in life, either consciously or subconsciously.

Taking a Test: Dreams of taking a test often signify feelings of being judged, evaluated, or unprepared for a situation in waking life. These dreams can indicate stress or anxiety about performance.

Being Late for Class: A dream where you're late for school or class can reflect feelings of inadequacy, missed opportunities, or the pressure to meet certain expectations.

Mountains and Valleys

Mountains and valleys are potent symbols of obstacles, goals, and emotional highs and lows.

Climbing a Mountain: Climbing a mountain in a dream may represent overcoming challenges or striving toward personal goals. The steepness of the mountain may reflect the difficulty of the journey.

Standing at the Top: Reaching the top of a mountain often symbolizes success, accomplishment, or a new perspective.

Valleys: Valleys may represent a period of rest, reflection, or low emotional energy, but they can also symbolize peace, safety, and renewal depending on the context of the dream.

Oceans, Lakes, and Rivers

Bodies of water, as explored in previous chapters, generally represent the dreamer's emotional state.

Ocean: The ocean represents the vastness of the subconscious and the unknown aspects of the dreamer's emotional life. Calm seas may symbolize peace and stability, while stormy seas reflect emotional turbulence.

River: A river often symbolizes the flow of life, the passage of time, or personal growth. Crossing a river might represent a major life transition, while being swept away by a river could indicate feeling overwhelmed by circumstances.

Lake: A lake, with its still, contained waters, might symbolize emotional reflection or a need to slow down and contemplate life's deeper meanings.

Cities and Towns

Cities in dreams often represent the complexities of life, social interactions, or the many different roles and responsibilities that the dreamer faces.

Busy City: A busy, bustling city can symbolize feelings of being overwhelmed by life's demands, responsibilities, or social interactions.

Abandoned City: An empty or abandoned city may indicate feelings of isolation or a desire for solitude. It can also symbolize neglect in certain areas of the dreamer's life.

Cemeteries

Cemeteries in dreams often symbolize endings, letting go, or transformation. They may indicate a need to process grief, accept change, or let go of something no longer serving the dreamer.

Walking Through a Cemetery: Walking through a cemetery might symbolize reflection on life, fear of death, or contemplating unresolved emotions from the past.

Seeing a Grave: Encountering a grave may indicate the need to bury the past or confront fears surrounding death and mortality.

Chapter 5: People in Dreams

People who appear in dreams can represent both themselves and different aspects of the dreamer's personality or psyche. Dreams involving people often explore the dreamer's relationships, attitudes, and unresolved emotional issues.

Family Members

Family members in dreams may represent the dreamer's real-life relationships, but they can also symbolize the influence of childhood and family dynamics on the dreamer's current life.

Parents: Dreaming of parents often symbolizes authority, guidance, or the need for support. A dream about a mother may involve nurturing, while a father may represent protection or responsibility.

Siblings: Siblings in dreams can represent rivalry, competition, or companionship. They may also symbolize qualities the dreamer associates with their sibling, such as strength or vulnerability.

Children: Children often represent innocence, vulnerability, or new beginnings. A dream of a child may indicate the dreamer's desire to nurture or protect someone—or aspects of themselves.

Friends

Friends in dreams often symbolize qualities or traits that the dreamer associates with those individuals. They may also reflect the dreamer's social connections, emotional support systems, or feelings of friendship and loyalty.

Close Friends: Dreams about close friends may reflect feelings of trust, emotional support, or shared experiences. They may also symbolize aspects of the dreamer's personality that resonate with the traits of that friend.

Former Friends: Dreaming of a former friend can represent nostalgia or unresolved emotions regarding a past relationship. It may also signal the dreamer's desire for closure or reconnection.

Strangers

Strangers in dreams often symbolize unknown or unfamiliar aspects of the dreamer's psyche. These figures may represent hidden desires, fears, or unexplored potential.

Unknown Figures: An unfamiliar person in a dream may symbolize a part of the dreamer that they do not yet recognize, such as talents, fears, or subconscious emotions.

Threatening Strangers: If a stranger appears menacing or threatening, this could indicate fear of the unknown or a repressed issue that the dreamer has not yet confronted.

Authority Figures

Authority figures, such as bosses, teachers, or police officers, often represent power, control, or discipline in dreams. They may also symbolize societal expectations or the dreamer's own internal standards.

Boss or Manager: A boss or manager in a dream may symbolize career concerns, stress about performance, or feelings of inadequacy in one's professional life.

Police Officer: A police officer can represent the dreamer's inner moral compass, their sense of right and wrong, or feelings of guilt and judgment.

Children and Babies

Children and babies in dreams can symbolize new beginnings, innocence, or vulnerability. They may also represent the dreamer's own inner child or creative potential.

Holding a Baby: Holding a baby in a dream often symbolizes a new responsibility, creative project, or aspect of the dreamer's life that requires nurturing.

Crying Baby: A crying baby might represent a neglected aspect of the dreamer's emotional needs or a project or responsibility that requires more attention.

Celebrities and Public Figures

Celebrities or public figures in dreams often represent idealized versions of success, fame, or power. They may also symbolize qualities or traits that the dreamer admires or aspires to.

Meeting a Celebrity: Dreaming of meeting a celebrity may reflect the dreamer's desire for recognition or the pursuit of success in a specific area of their life.

Becoming Famous: Becoming famous in a dream may symbolize the dreamer's need for validation, acknowledgment, or a desire to be seen and appreciated.

Chapter 6: Actions and Experiences in Dreams

The actions and experiences that occur in dreams—whether flying, falling, or being chased—can provide deep insights into the dreamer's emotional state, fears, and desires.

Flying

Flying in dreams often symbolizes freedom, escape, or a heightened sense of awareness. The experience of flying can evoke feelings of liberation, control, or transcendence.

Flying Freely: Flying freely through the sky may symbolize a sense of empowerment, personal freedom, or a desire to rise above limitations.

Struggling to Fly: Difficulty in flying or feeling weighed down while flying may reflect the dreamer's struggles with self-confidence or fear of failure.

Falling

Falling in dreams is a common experience and is often associated with feelings of insecurity, fear, or loss of control.

Falling from a Great Height: This can indicate fear of failure, anxiety about taking risks, or concern over losing stability in one's life.

Landing Safely: Safely landing after a fall may suggest resilience or the ability to recover from setbacks.

Chasing and Being Chased

Dreams of being chased often symbolize avoidance of a problem, fear of confrontation, or unresolved stress. The person or object chasing the dreamer may represent a fear or issue that needs addressing.

Running Away: If the dreamer is running away from the pursuer, it may indicate that they are avoiding confronting a difficult situation or emotion.

Turning to Face the Pursuer: Facing the person or creature chasing you can symbolize courage, resolution, or the desire to confront an issue head-on.

Being Trapped

Dreams of being trapped, whether in a small space or a complicated situation, often reflect feelings of helplessness or being stuck in waking life.

Stuck in a Maze: A dream of being stuck in a maze may represent confusion, indecision, or the inability to find a way out of a difficult situation.

Locked in a Room: Being locked in a room can symbolize feelings of isolation, restriction, or a fear of being confined or controlled.

Losing Something

Losing objects or people in dreams can symbolize fear of loss, insecurity, or unresolved feelings about change.

Lost Object: Losing a valuable object may represent feelings of inadequacy or fear of losing something important in waking life.

Lost Person: Searching for a lost person may indicate emotional detachment or a longing for reconnection with someone significant in the dreamer's life.

Finding Something New

Finding something in a dream often symbolizes discovering new opportunities, talents, or insights. It can represent the arrival of something unexpected but valuable in the dreamer's life.

Finding a Key: Discovering a key in a dream often symbolizes unlocking new opportunities, understanding, or gaining access to previously hidden knowledge.

Finding Money: Finding money may represent feelings of abundance, self-worth, or the discovery of untapped potential.

Chapter 7: Dream Themes and Motifs

Dreams often contain recurring themes or motifs that symbolize significant life issues or emotional states. These themes may appear across different dream settings, characters, and symbols. Understanding these recurring dream themes can help reveal deeper insights into the dreamer's inner world.

Death and Rebirth

Dreams about death are common and are often misunderstood as negative or ominous. However, death in dreams typically symbolizes transformation, the end of one phase of life, and the beginning of another.

Dreaming of Your Own Death: This may reflect a desire for personal transformation, such as ending bad habits or moving on from a particular phase in life.

Seeing Someone Else Die: Seeing someone else die may represent the dreamer's perception of change in their relationship with that person or indicate that the dreamer is moving on from an influence they've had.

Rebirth: Dreams of rebirth, such as witnessing someone being born or rising from the dead, symbolize new beginnings, growth, and renewal.

Transformation and Metamorphosis

Transformation dreams involve a dramatic shift in the dreamer's identity, environment, or physical form. These types of dreams symbolize personal growth, adaptation, and the dreamer's ability to navigate life changes.

Changing Into Another Person or Creature: Becoming someone or something else in a dream often represents the dreamer's changing identity or how they perceive themselves in different roles.

Objects Transforming: When objects or environments transform, it often reflects changing attitudes or the dreamer's evolving perspective on certain issues.

Facing Fear

Dreams that center around confronting fears or anxieties allow the dreamer to symbolically work through difficult emotions or unresolved stressors.

Confronting a Monster: Facing a monster or dangerous creature in a dream may symbolize the dreamer's attempt to deal with suppressed fears or trauma.

Surviving a Threat: Dreams in which the dreamer survives an attack or threatening situation often reflect personal resilience or the desire to overcome challenges in waking life.

Love and Relationships

Dreams about love, romance, and relationships often mirror the dreamer's real-life emotional state or desires, as well as subconscious fears or unresolved issues within their relationships.

Falling in Love: Dreaming of falling in love may reflect the dreamer's desire for emotional connection or intimacy.

Relationship Conflict: Dreams of arguments or breakups may symbolize inner conflicts about the relationship or unresolved tension that the dreamer is processing subconsciously.

Reuniting with an Ex: Dreaming of a former romantic partner may indicate unresolved emotions about the past relationship, or it may symbolize a need to integrate aspects of oneself that were left behind.

Conflict and Resolution

Conflict in dreams often symbolizes inner turmoil, tension in relationships, or a struggle to reconcile opposing desires or emotions. The way these conflicts are resolved in the dream can offer insights into the dreamer's ability to cope with challenges in waking life.

Physical Fights: Physical altercations in dreams can represent personal struggles, either with oneself or others. They may also symbolize a desire for power or control over a situation.

Negotiation or Peace-Making: Resolving a conflict peacefully in a dream may indicate the dreamer's readiness to resolve personal or interpersonal issues in waking life.

Success and Failure

Dreams about success and failure often reflect the dreamer's aspirations, insecurities, or fears about real-life endeavors.

Achieving a Goal: Dreams in which the dreamer achieves something significant—such as winning a race, receiving an award, or finishing a project—often symbolize feelings of accomplishment or a desire for recognition.

Failing a Test: Failure dreams, such as failing an exam or losing a competition, usually symbolize feelings of inadequacy, fear of failure, or anxiety about being judged.

Chapter 8: Interpreting Your Own Dreams

Dream interpretation is an intensely personal process, as symbols, settings, and characters may hold different meanings for each individual. In this chapter, we guide you through techniques for understanding your own dreams and developing a deeper connection with your subconscious mind.

Keeping a Dream Journal

A dream journal is an essential tool for tracking and interpreting your dreams over time. By recording dreams as soon as you wake up, you can better capture details that may be forgotten later.

Why a Dream Journal Matters: Writing down your dreams helps you notice patterns, recurring symbols, and emotional themes. These patterns can offer insight into unresolved issues or areas of growth.

How to Start: Keep a notebook by your bed and make it a habit to write down your dreams as soon as you wake up. Even if you only remember fragments, capturing those details can be key to understanding the bigger picture.

How to Remember Your Dreams

Dream recall can be difficult, especially for people who don't actively try to remember their dreams. However, there are methods to improve dream recall.

Establish a Pre-Sleep Routine: Before falling asleep, tell yourself that you will remember your dreams. This intention-setting primes the mind for dream recall.

Wake Up Slowly: When you wake up, remain still for a few moments to allow yourself to recall your dreams. Moving too quickly can disrupt the fragile memory of the dream.

Using Dream Dictionaries Effectively

Dream dictionaries can provide valuable starting points for interpreting symbols, but they should be used as guides rather than definitive answers.

Personalizing Dream Symbols: While some symbols have common meanings, your personal experiences and emotions will influence how you interpret your dreams. For example, a snake may symbolize fear to some, but to others, it may represent healing or wisdom.

Combining Dictionary and Intuition: Use the symbolic interpretations from dream dictionaries as a foundation, but rely on your own intuition and emotional response to truly decode your dreams.

Dream Meditation Techniques

Meditation can be a powerful tool for delving deeper into the meaning of your dreams. It allows you to focus on specific dream symbols or experiences and explore what they represent at a subconscious level.

Meditating on Dream Symbols: Focus on a specific symbol from your dream (such as a key, door, or animal) and meditate on its potential meanings. Allow images, feelings, or associations to arise naturally as you explore the symbol in your waking mind.

Guided Dream Meditation: Some meditative techniques guide you back into the dream state while you're awake, enabling you to ask questions about the dream's meaning and explore it more deeply.

Understanding Personal Symbols

While some symbols have universal meanings, others are deeply personal and may require the dreamer to reflect on their own life experiences to decode their significance.

Identifying Personal Symbols: Pay attention to recurring symbols in your dreams and their connection to your waking life. For instance, a childhood home may symbolize safety and nostalgia, while a specific person may represent a part of your personality or a life lesson.

Symbol Associations: Consider what each symbol makes you feel or remember. These associations often hold the key to the dream's deeper meaning.

Chapter 9: Advanced Dream Analysis

Once you've developed the habit of journaling your dreams and interpreting them through symbols and themes, you can dive deeper into advanced dream analysis techniques. These methods often involve psychology, archetypal exploration, and even therapeutic applications.

Archetypes in Dreams (Jungian Approach)

Carl Jung's theory of archetypes offers a powerful framework for interpreting dreams. Archetypes are universal symbols and patterns that recur in dreams and myths across cultures and time periods.

The Shadow: The shadow archetype represents the unconscious aspects of ourselves that we repress or deny. When the shadow appears in dreams, it often takes the form of a menacing figure, urging the dreamer to confront hidden fears or desires.

The Hero: The hero archetype symbolizes the dreamer's journey of personal growth and triumph over adversity. A dream in which the dreamer becomes a hero may indicate personal strength or the desire to overcome obstacles.

The Anima/Animus: These represent the feminine and masculine aspects of the psyche. Dreams involving the anima or animus may indicate a need to integrate these opposing forces within the dreamer's personality.

Shadow Work and Dreams

Dreams are a prime vehicle for engaging in shadow work, a process of exploring and integrating the hidden, often uncomfortable parts of ourselves.

Exploring the Shadow Self: Dreams in which the dreamer faces their own negative qualities or darker impulses offer opportunities for self-acceptance and personal growth.

How to Use Dreams for Shadow Work: Reflect on dreams that evoke discomfort, fear, or guilt. These emotions often point to repressed parts of the self that need acknowledgment and healing.

Dreams as Problem Solvers

Dreams frequently serve as a tool for solving problems or working through emotional dilemmas. The brain processes information differently during sleep, allowing for creative solutions that may not be apparent in waking life.

Analyzing Problem-Solving Dreams: Pay attention to dreams that seem to offer solutions or insight into real-life issues. The way you navigate challenges in dreams can mirror how you approach them in waking life.

Dream Incubation: Dream incubation is a technique that involves focusing on a specific problem or question before falling asleep in hopes of receiving a solution through a dream.

Connecting Dreams to Waking Life

Understanding how dreams relate to waking life can deepen self-awareness and help the dreamer better navigate real-life challenges.

Symbolic Reflections: Consider how the symbols in your dreams reflect your waking concerns. For instance, a dream about drowning may reflect feelings of being overwhelmed by responsibilities in waking life.

Applying Dream Insights: Use the insights gained from dreams to address unresolved issues, make decisions, or navigate relationships more effectively.

The Collective Unconscious and Shared Dreams

The collective unconscious refers to a set of shared symbols and experiences common to all humanity, as proposed by Jung. Shared or similar dreams across different people may point to universal concerns, such as death, fear of failure, or the pursuit of love.

Shared Dream Themes: Themes like flying, falling, and being chased occur frequently in dreams across cultures, indicating their deep connection to the collective unconscious.

Interpreting Shared Dreams: If multiple people experience similar dreams, it may suggest they are collectively processing a significant event or emotional state, such as grief or anticipation.

Chapter 12: Dream Interpretation Dictionary

This comprehensive dream dictionary provides detailed interpretations of common dream symbols. Each symbol is explored from multiple angles, offering psychological, spiritual, and cultural meanings. Keep in mind that dream symbols are deeply personal, and while this dictionary provides general insights, the true meaning of a symbol depends on the dreamer's individual context and emotional state.

A

Air: Represents thoughts, ideas, and intellect. Dreaming of air can suggest a need for clarity, freedom, or spiritual awareness.

Calm Air: Signifies peace of mind and mental clarity.

Windy Air: Suggests turmoil in thoughts or the need to adapt to changes in life.

Airplane: Symbolizes a journey, ambition, or the desire to achieve new heights in life.

Taking Off: Indicates new ventures or a transition in life.

Crash: Reflects fears of failure, loss of control, or anxiety about reaching goals.

Anchor: Represents stability, grounding, and security.

Secured Anchor: Indicates a feeling of being grounded and stable in life.

Lost Anchor: Suggests feelings of insecurity or being adrift without direction.

Angel: Symbolizes protection, guidance, or a divine message. Angels often appear in dreams to offer reassurance or spiritual insight.

Talking Angel: Suggests the need to listen to inner wisdom or intuition.

Falling Angel: Indicates a loss of faith, spiritual crisis, or a need for redemption.

B

Baby: Represents innocence, new beginnings, or vulnerability. A baby in a dream often reflects something new in the dreamer's life that needs care and nurturing.

Holding a Baby: Symbolizes a new responsibility or project.

Crying Baby: Suggests neglected responsibilities or emotional needs that require attention.

Bicycle: Symbolizes balance, personal progress, and self-reliance. Dreaming of riding a bicycle suggests that the dreamer is moving through life at their own pace, often balancing multiple aspects of life.

Riding Smoothly: Indicates that life is in balance and moving forward harmoniously.

Falling Off: Represents challenges in maintaining stability or control in personal life.

Bird: Represents freedom, aspirations, and the soul. Birds in dreams often symbolize the desire to rise above limitations or escape from life's challenges.

Flying Bird: Suggests personal freedom or a desire to reach new heights.

Caged Bird: Reflects feelings of confinement or restriction in one's life.

Bridge: Symbolizes transition, connection, or a passage from one phase of life to another.

Crossing a Bridge: Represents a life change or the desire to overcome an obstacle.

Broken Bridge: Suggests difficulties in moving forward or fear of the unknown.

C

Car: Represents control, direction, and autonomy in life. The state of the car in a dream often reflects the dreamer's ability to navigate life's journey.

Driving a Car: Symbolizes control over one's path in life.

Out of Control Car: Reflects feelings of losing control or direction.

Castle: Represents protection, wealth, and personal power. Castles in dreams can also symbolize aspirations or the desire for security.

Entering a Castle: Indicates a journey into the self or pursuit of one's ambitions.

Abandoned Castle: Suggests unfulfilled goals or a sense of lost potential.

Cat: Symbolizes independence, intuition, and mystery. Cats often reflect the dreamer's relationship with their own instincts and desires.

Friendly Cat: Represents comfort with one's intuitive or independent side.

Aggressive Cat: Suggests suppressed anger or feelings of vulnerability.

Cave: Symbolizes the subconscious mind, hidden truths, or personal introspection.

Entering a Cave: Represents the exploration of hidden aspects of oneself.

Being Trapped in a Cave: Reflects feelings of being stuck in one's own thoughts or emotions.

D

Death: Represents transformation, endings, and new beginnings. Dreaming of death often symbolizes major changes in life rather than literal death.

Dying: Indicates personal transformation or the end of a life phase.

Seeing Someone Else Die: Reflects changes in the dreamer's relationship with that person or a part of themselves that they associate with that individual.

Dog: Symbolizes loyalty, friendship, and protection. Dogs in dreams often reflect the dreamer's relationships with others or their own loyalty.

Friendly Dog: Represents loyalty and trust in relationships.

Aggressive Dog: Suggests conflict, betrayal, or fear of confrontation.

Door: Symbolizes opportunities, choices, and transitions. Doors in dreams often represent the opening or closing of opportunities.

Open Door: Suggests new possibilities or the start of a new phase in life.

Closed Door: Reflects missed opportunities or barriers to progress.

Dragon: Represents power, strength, or a formidable challenge. Dragons may also symbolize repressed emotions or the shadow side of the psyche.

Taming a Dragon: Reflects mastery over one's fears or emotions.

Fighting a Dragon: Represents confrontation with a significant life challenge.

E

Earthquake: Represents upheaval, instability, and sudden change. Dreaming of an earthquake often reflects feelings of uncertainty or fear of life's unpredictability.

Surviving an Earthquake: Suggests resilience and adaptability in the face of change.

Being Buried: Reflects feelings of being overwhelmed or trapped by circumstances.

Egg: Symbolizes potential, creation, and new beginnings. An egg in a dream often reflects the dreamer's potential for growth or the start of something new.

Cracking an Egg: Represents the birth of new ideas or opportunities.

Broken Egg: Suggests lost potential or disappointment.

Elephant: Represents strength, wisdom, and memory. Dreaming of an elephant often suggests that the dreamer is dealing with deep emotions or long-term issues.

Riding an Elephant: Reflects mastery over strong emotions or life challenges.

Aggressive Elephant: Suggests a problem or issue that is overwhelming or too large to handle.

F

Falling: Symbolizes loss of control, insecurity, or fear of failure. Falling dreams often occur during times of anxiety or stress.

Falling from a Height: Reflects fear of losing status or control in life.

Landing Safely: Suggests resilience or the ability to recover from setbacks.

Fire: Represents passion, transformation, destruction, or purification.

Controlled Fire: Suggests personal power or a desire for transformation.

Out-of-Control Fire: Reflects overwhelming emotions, anger, or a destructive situation in life.

Fish: Symbolizes fertility, creativity, and unconscious thoughts. Fish in dreams often represent ideas or emotions that are surfacing from the subconscious.

Catching a Fish: Reflects the discovery of hidden talents or ideas.

Dead Fish: Suggests missed opportunities or lost potential.

Forest: Represents the unconscious, mystery, and exploration of hidden aspects of the self.

Lost in a Forest: Reflects feelings of confusion or being overwhelmed by unconscious emotions.

Walking Through a Forest: Suggests a journey of self-discovery or personal growth.

G

Ghost: Symbolizes unresolved issues, memories, or emotions. Ghosts in dreams often reflect past experiences that continue to haunt the dreamer.

Talking to a Ghost: Suggests a need to confront unresolved issues or past traumas.

Being Chased by a Ghost: Reflects feelings of guilt or fear of the past.

Gold: Represents wealth, success, and spiritual enlightenment. Dreaming of gold often suggests the dreamer is discovering something valuable within themselves.

Finding Gold: Reflects self-discovery or a new opportunity for success.

Losing Gold: Suggests fear of losing something valuable or missing out on an opportunity.

Garden: Symbolizes personal growth, peace, and abundance. Gardens in dreams often reflect the dreamer's inner state of mind or emotional well-being.

Tending to a Garden: Represents nurturing personal or emotional growth.

Overgrown Garden: Suggests neglect of personal issues or emotional health.

H

Hair: Represents strength, identity, and personal power.

Cutting Hair: Reflects a desire for change, transformation, or feelings of vulnerability.

Losing Hair: Suggests fear of aging or loss of vitality.

Horse: Symbolizes freedom, power, and instinct.

Riding a Horse: Represents personal power and control over one's life direction.

Wild Horse: Suggests untamed emotions or desires that need to be acknowledged or controlled.

House: Represents the self and different aspects of the dreamer's life.

New House: Symbolizes personal growth or a new phase in life.

Old or Broken House: Reflects neglected areas of life or unresolved emotional issues.

Hurricane: Symbolizes emotional turmoil, overwhelming forces, or major life changes.

Surviving a Hurricane: Reflects resilience and the ability to weather emotional or life storms.

Being Swept Away: Suggests feeling overwhelmed by powerful emotions or uncontrollable events.

I

Ice: Symbolizes frozen emotions, rigidity, or feeling stuck in life.

Walking on Ice: Reflects caution in dealing with emotional or personal issues.

Falling Through Ice: Suggests vulnerability or being overwhelmed by suppressed emotions.

Island: Represents isolation, self-sufficiency, or a desire for solitude.

Stranded on an Island: Reflects feelings of loneliness or separation from others.

Peaceful Island: Suggests a need for relaxation or personal reflection.

Injury: Represents vulnerability, weakness, or emotional wounds.

Injuring Someone Else: Suggests feelings of guilt or fear of harming others emotionally.

Being Injured: Reflects a fear of being hurt or feelings of inadequacy.

J

Jewelry: Symbolizes self-worth, value, and personal achievements.

Receiving Jewelry: Suggests recognition of personal value or a reward.

Losing Jewelry: Reflects feelings of insecurity or fear of losing status or personal worth.

Journey: Represents personal growth, self-discovery, or life transitions.

Starting a Journey: Reflects embarking on a new phase in life or personal development.

Lost on a Journey: Suggests feelings of confusion or lack of direction in life.

K

Key: Symbolizes access, knowledge, or solutions.

Finding a Key: Reflects discovering a solution or unlocking hidden potential.

Losing a Key: Suggests fear of missed opportunities or a sense of helplessness.

Knife: Represents conflict, separation, or decisive action.

Holding a Knife: Suggests a need to confront an issue or take decisive action.

Being Stabbed: Reflects feelings of betrayal or fear of being hurt emotionally.

L

Labyrinth: Represents confusion, complexity, and the search for solutions.

Navigating a Labyrinth: Reflects working through a complex situation or emotional struggle.

Lost in a Labyrinth: Suggests feeling overwhelmed by life's challenges or emotional entanglements.

Lion: Symbolizes strength, courage, and leadership.

Taming a Lion: Reflects control over powerful emotions or mastering a challenge.

Attacked by a Lion: Suggests feeling threatened by a powerful force in life.

Light: Represents clarity, awareness, and enlightenment.

Bright Light: Suggests gaining new insight or understanding in life.

Dim or Flickering Light: Reflects confusion, uncertainty, or lack of clarity in a situation.

M

Mountain: Symbolizes challenges, aspirations, and personal growth.

Climbing a Mountain: Reflects overcoming obstacles or striving toward a goal.

At the Top of a Mountain: Suggests success, accomplishment, or a new perspective on life.

Mirror: Symbolizes self-reflection, identity, and truth.

Looking in a Mirror: Reflects self-examination or the need to see oneself clearly.

Broken Mirror: Suggests insecurity, fear of the truth, or shattered identity.

Money: Represents value, self-worth, and resources.

Finding Money: Reflects new opportunities or increased self-esteem.

Losing Money: Suggests fear of financial instability or feelings of inadequacy.

N

Night: Represents mystery, the unconscious, or hidden aspects of the self.

Walking in the Night: Reflects navigating unknown aspects of life or subconscious emotions.

Fear of the Night: Suggests fear of the unknown or unresolved emotions lurking beneath the surface.

Nest: Symbolizes safety, security, and family.

Bird's Nest: Reflects the dreamer's need for security or a nurturing environment.

Empty Nest: Suggests feelings of abandonment, loneliness, or a major life transition (e.g., children leaving home).

O

Ocean: Represents emotions, the subconscious, and the vastness of life.

Calm Ocean: Reflects emotional peace and stability.

Stormy Ocean: Suggests emotional turmoil, fear, or feelings of being overwhelmed.

Owl: Symbolizes wisdom, intuition, and hidden knowledge.

Seeing an Owl: Reflects the need for wisdom or insight in a situation.

Hearing an Owl: Suggests a message from the subconscious or a warning of impending change.

P

Path: Symbolizes life's journey, choices, and direction.

Straight Path: Reflects clarity and a clear direction in life.

Twisting Path: Suggests uncertainty or complex decisions ahead.

Prison: Symbolizes feelings of restriction, confinement, or being trapped.

In Prison: Reflects feelings of being trapped in a situation or relationship.

Escaping Prison: Suggests a desire for freedom or breaking free from limitations.

Phoenix: Symbolizes rebirth, transformation, and renewal.

Rising Phoenix: Reflects overcoming adversity or a significant life transformation.

Burning Phoenix: Suggests letting go of the past to make way for new growth.

Q

Quicksand: Symbolizes danger, instability, or feelings of being overwhelmed.

Sinking in Quicksand: Reflects feelings of being stuck or pulled down by a situation in life.

Escaping Quicksand: Suggests the ability to overcome difficult challenges.

R

Rainbow: Symbolizes hope, renewal, and divine promise.

Seeing a Rainbow: Reflects optimism and the resolution of difficulties.

Chasing a Rainbow: Suggests pursuing unattainable goals or ideals.

River: Represents the flow of life, emotions, and the passage of time.

Crossing a River: Suggests a significant life transition or emotional journey.

Drowning in a River: Reflects feelings of being overwhelmed by emotions.

S

Snake: Represents transformation, healing, or hidden fears. In some cultures, snakes are also seen as symbols of wisdom and fertility.

Friendly Snake: Reflects personal growth or the healing process.

Venomous Snake: Suggests danger, betrayal, or fear of someone in waking life.

Star: Symbolizes hope, inspiration, and guidance.

Bright Star: Reflects guidance or a source of inspiration in life.

Falling Star: Suggests lost hope or disappointment in a goal.

Sword: Represents conflict, power, or decisiveness.

Wielding a Sword: Reflects personal strength or the ability to cut through obstacles.

Broken Sword: Suggests feelings of powerlessness or failure in a conflict.

T

Teeth: Symbolizes communication, power, and confidence. Dreams about teeth are often related to feelings of vulnerability or insecurity.

Losing Teeth: Reflects anxiety about self-image or fear of aging.

Healthy Teeth: Suggests confidence and strong communication skills.

Tiger: Represents power, passion, and raw instinct.

Tame Tiger: Reflects control over one's instincts or passions.

Aggressive Tiger: Suggests fear of one's primal urges or a powerful adversary in life.

Tree: Symbolizes growth, stability, and personal development.

Climbing a Tree: Reflects striving for personal growth or higher knowledge.

Falling Tree: Suggests fear of loss or instability in life.

U

Umbrella: Symbolizes protection, security, and preparedness.

Using an Umbrella: Reflects the need for emotional protection or shielding oneself from life's difficulties.

Broken Umbrella: Suggests feelings of vulnerability or lack of protection.

Unicorn: Symbolizes purity, magic, and the pursuit of ideals.

Seeing a Unicorn: Reflects a desire for innocence, purity, or the fulfillment of dreams.

Chasing a Unicorn: Suggests pursuing unattainable ideals or perfection.

V

Volcano: Represents explosive emotions, repressed anger, or impending change.

Erupting Volcano: Reflects a release of pent-up emotions or a major life upheaval.

Dormant Volcano: Suggests unresolved issues or emotions that are waiting to surface.

Vase: Symbolizes containment, beauty, and hidden emotions.

Full Vase: Reflects fulfillment or emotional abundance.

Broken Vase: Suggests loss, broken trust, or emotional vulnerability.

W

Waterfall: Symbolizes emotional release, cleansing, and transformation.

Standing Under a Waterfall: Reflects personal cleansing or the release of emotions.

Watching a Waterfall: Suggests observing emotional changes or feeling awe at life's flow.

Wings: Symbolizes freedom, transcendence, and spiritual growth.

Flying with Wings: Reflects personal freedom or the desire to rise above limitations.

Broken Wings: Suggests feelings of being held back or limited in life.

Window: Symbolizes perspective, opportunities, and clarity.

Looking Out a Window: Reflects the dreamer's outlook on life or the search for new opportunities.

Closed Window: Suggests missed opportunities or feeling trapped.

X

X-Ray: Symbolizes insight, seeing beyond the surface, or uncovering hidden truths.

Receiving an X-Ray: Reflects the desire for deeper understanding or clarity in a situation.

Seeing Inside Someone with an X-Ray: Suggests gaining insight into someone's true nature or hidden motives.

Y

Yacht: Symbolizes luxury, success, and personal achievement.

Sailing a Yacht: Reflects confidence in navigating life's challenges and the pursuit of success.

Sinking Yacht: Suggests fear of losing success or control over life's direction.

Z

Zoo: Symbolizes containment of emotions, instincts, or desires.

Visiting a Zoo: Reflects the desire to observe or control one's emotions or instincts.

Escaping Animals from a Zoo: Suggests repressed emotions or instincts breaking free and causing disruption.

This dream dictionary provides a comprehensive reference for interpreting the symbols that commonly appear in dreams. As always, personal experiences, emotions, and contexts play a significant role in understanding the true meaning behind each symbol. Dreamers are encouraged to use this dictionary as a guide while reflecting on their own life situations for deeper insights.

Chapter 13: Frequently Asked Questions (FAQ)

In this chapter, we address common questions about dreams and dream interpretation. These questions often arise for those trying to understand the meanings behind their dreams, and the answers provide clarity and guidance for dreamers seeking to deepen their connection with their subconscious mind.

Can dreams predict the future?

Many people believe in the possibility of prophetic dreams—those that seem to foretell future events. While there are anecdotal accounts of individuals dreaming about significant events before they happen, scientific evidence supporting the idea of dreams as future predictors is limited.

Dreams are more likely to reflect the dreamer's thoughts, emotions, and concerns, allowing them to process potential outcomes or scenarios. In this sense, dreams can sometimes seem predictive because they help us subconsciously prepare for situations. However, most researchers agree that dreams do not directly predict the future, though they may offer intuitive insights based on what the dreamer already knows.

Why do I keep having the same dream?

Recurring dreams usually indicate unresolved issues or patterns in your waking life that you haven't addressed. These dreams persist because your subconscious is trying to draw attention to something you're ignoring or suppressing. The recurring nature suggests that the dream's message is important, and the dream will continue until the underlying issue is confronted.

Some common themes in recurring dreams include:

Being chased

Falling

Unpreparedness for an exam or event

Losing teeth

To stop the recurring dream, focus on identifying the issue it reflects and work to resolve it in your waking life. Keeping a dream journal may help you track the patterns and emotions tied to these dreams.

Are nightmares dangerous?

Nightmares themselves are not dangerous, but they can be distressing, especially if they are frequent or intense. Nightmares often arise from anxiety, fear, or trauma, serving as the brain's way of processing difficult emotions or experiences. While nightmares can be uncomfortable, they offer insight into unresolved issues.

For individuals with post-traumatic stress disorder (PTSD) or other conditions, chronic nightmares may disrupt sleep and contribute to mental health struggles. Techniques like dream rehearsal therapy, where you practice changing the ending of a nightmare while awake, or working through traumatic experiences with a therapist can help alleviate recurring nightmares.

Do dream symbols have universal meanings?

While some dream symbols, like water, flying, or teeth, seem to have universal associations across cultures, dream interpretation is highly personal. Symbols may have different meanings depending on your life experiences, beliefs, and emotional state.

For example, a snake may symbolize danger for one person but transformation and healing for another, depending on their cultural or personal associations with snakes.

Universal symbols, also called archetypes (such as those identified by Carl Jung), do exist and can represent collective human experiences, but always consider your own context when interpreting dreams.

Why do we forget dreams so easily?

Dreams often fade from memory quickly because the brain deprioritizes them during the transition from sleep to waking consciousness. The brain shifts its focus to conscious activities, causing dream memories to disappear unless they are recalled immediately after waking. Additionally, the part of the brain responsible for creating and storing long-term memories is less active during sleep, which contributes to dream amnesia.

To improve dream recall:

Keep a notebook by your bed to write down dreams as soon as you wake up.

Wake up slowly and remain still for a few moments, giving yourself time to remember your dreams before engaging with the day.

Set an intention before bed to remember your dreams.

Why do we have nightmares?

Nightmares occur when the brain processes intense emotions like fear, stress, or unresolved trauma during sleep. Common causes of nightmares include:

Stress or anxiety from life events

Traumatic experiences (especially for those with PTSD)

Sleep disorders like sleep apnea

Certain medications

Substance use or withdrawal

Nightmares serve an important function in helping us cope with distressing feelings and situations. Although unpleasant, they offer valuable insight into unresolved emotions or fears that need attention. Addressing the source of the stress or trauma can reduce the frequency and intensity of nightmares.

Can I control my dreams?

Yes, lucid dreaming allows dreamers to become aware that they are dreaming and, in some cases, control their dreams. Lucid dreaming occurs when the dreamer realizes they are in a dream state and can influence the narrative, characters, and environment.

Techniques for inducing lucid dreams include:

Reality checks: Throughout the day, ask yourself if you're dreaming by checking your surroundings or attempting to perform a simple task (like reading text or looking at your hands).

Dream journaling: Writing down your dreams can help improve dream recall and increase awareness within your dreams.

Mnemonic Induction of Lucid Dreams (MILD): Before sleeping, tell yourself that you will recognize when you're dreaming, and repeat this intention until you fall asleep.

With practice, you can use lucid dreams for personal exploration, creativity, or even overcoming fears.

Do people in my dreams represent themselves or parts of me?

The people who appear in your dreams can represent both themselves and aspects of your own psyche. In some cases, they symbolize qualities or emotions you associate with them. For example, dreaming about a close friend may represent a part of yourself that is compassionate, fun-loving, or independent.

At other times, characters in dreams reflect parts of you that you may not recognize or are struggling with. For example, an authority figure might symbolize your own internal rules or restrictions. Jungian psychology suggests that every figure in a dream represents an aspect of the dreamer's unconscious mind.

Chapter 14: Dreaming of the Deceased

Dreaming of deceased family members and friends is a common experience and can hold deep emotional and psychological significance. These dreams often serve multiple functions, reflecting the dreamer's emotional processing, unresolved feelings, or even a desire for connection. Here are some potential reasons why you might continue dreaming of loved ones who have passed away:

1. Emotional Healing and Grief Processing

When a loved one dies, the grieving process doesn't end with their passing. Dreams of deceased family and friends can be part of your ongoing process of grief and healing. The subconscious mind uses dreams as a way to process unresolved emotions, including sorrow, guilt, or unfinished conversations. In these dreams, you may be revisiting memories, seeking closure, or coming to terms with their absence.

Dreams as a Safe Space for Healing: Dreams allow you to confront feelings of loss in a way that might feel too overwhelming in waking life. These dreams may provide an opportunity to say goodbye, express unspoken emotions, or simply feel connected to the person again.

2. Unresolved Issues or Unfinished Business

Sometimes, dreams of deceased loved ones reflect unresolved issues or "unfinished business" that you may have with that person. This could include lingering feelings of guilt, regret, or things left unsaid. These dreams provide a space where your subconscious mind attempts to resolve these emotions.

Dreams as Conversations: In dreams, you may find yourself having conversations with the deceased, seeking forgiveness, or clarifying something left unresolved. Your subconscious mind may be working to find closure and peace by bringing up these relationships.

3. Desire for Connection

Dreams of the deceased often occur when we deeply miss someone and wish to feel connected to them again. These dreams can be comforting, as they allow you to interact with the loved one in a way that feels real, offering a sense of closeness or protection.

Emotional Comfort: Your mind may create these dreams to give you the experience of interacting with the deceased, which can bring comfort during difficult times. These dreams may happen more frequently during periods of stress, change, or emotional need, when you subconsciously seek their presence for guidance or reassurance.

4. Symbolic Representation

In some cases, deceased family members and friends may represent aspects of your own psyche or personal traits associated with them. For example, a mother or father figure in a dream might symbolize protection, guidance, or life lessons that you are reflecting on.

Internalized Wisdom: The appearance of a deceased loved one in a dream can symbolize the part of yourself that embodies their qualities. If you dream of a family member who was known for being wise or protective, your subconscious may be calling upon those qualities in yourself or your current situation.

5. Processing Life Transitions

Deceased loved ones often appear in dreams during times of personal change or transition, such as a new job, a relationship shift, or a major life decision. These dreams may reflect your subconscious working through the advice, values, or guidance that these individuals gave you during their life, especially when you are facing uncertainty or need support.

Seeking Guidance: Even though they are no longer physically present, these loved ones might appear in your dreams as a source of guidance, helping you navigate challenges or reinforcing the lessons they imparted to you.

6. Spiritual or Mystical Interpretation

In some spiritual traditions, dreams of deceased loved ones are seen as visitations or messages from the afterlife. For those who believe in an afterlife or spiritual realm, these dreams may be viewed as a form of communication from the deceased, offering comfort, protection, or insight.

Visitations: You may interpret these dreams as the loved one reaching out to offer reassurance or letting you know they are still with you in spirit. For some, these dreams feel vivid or emotionally charged, contributing to the belief that the loved one's presence is more than just symbolic.

7. Coping with Mortality

Dreams of the deceased can also reflect your own contemplation of mortality and the cycle of life. These dreams may prompt you to reflect on the impermanence of life, your own experiences of death, or the legacies left behind by those you have lost.

Facing Mortality: Dreaming of someone who has died can bring thoughts of your own life and mortality to the surface, urging you to reflect on how you're living, what matters most, and how you want to honor the people you have lost.

How to Approach These Dreams:

Reflect on Emotions: Consider how you feel during and after the dream. Are you comforted, anxious, or unsettled? The emotional tone of the dream may provide clues about what your subconscious is processing.

Journal Your Dreams: Writing down your dreams can help you identify patterns, emotions, or unresolved feelings that may be linked to the deceased. This practice can bring clarity and aid in emotional processing.

Seek Closure: If your dreams suggest unresolved issues, consider ways to address these in your waking life, whether through reflection, speaking with loved ones, or even writing a letter to the deceased (as a symbolic form of communication).

Accept the Message: If the dreams are comforting and feel like visitations, embrace them as moments of connection and reassurance, especially during difficult times.

Ultimately, dreams of deceased family members and friends are a natural part of emotional processing and healing. They offer an opportunity to continue your relationship with the memory of those you've lost, allowing you to navigate feelings of grief, love, and transformation in the safety of the dream world.

Chapter 15: Final Thoughts

Dreams are a rich, multifaceted experience, offering deep insights into our inner worlds. They reflect our emotions, desires, fears, and hopes, serving as a bridge between the conscious and unconscious mind. Whether you believe dreams are messages from the divine, reflections of psychological processes, or glimpses of the future, there is no denying their power and mystery.

As you've journeyed through this book, you've explored the many dimensions of dream interpretation. You've learned to recognize common symbols, understand personal and universal meanings, and apply these insights to your own life. Dream interpretation is not just about finding meaning in abstract images—it's about personal growth, self-awareness, and healing. By:

Keeping a Dream Journal: You capture the fleeting images and emotions from your dreams, helping you identify patterns and recurring themes. This practice allows you to see connections between your dreams and your waking life.

Listening to Your Subconscious: Your dreams are a direct line to your unconscious thoughts and feelings. Paying attention to them can help you resolve conflicts, overcome fears, and pursue your deepest desires.

Engaging with Dream Symbols: As you decode the language of your dreams, you become more attuned to the unique symbolism of your personal experiences, allowing you to discover insights that resonate with your inner truth.

The Journey Continues

Dream interpretation is not a one-time practice—it is a lifelong journey. As you grow, your dreams will evolve, reflecting new challenges, triumphs, and personal discoveries. By maintaining an open dialogue with your dreams, you empower yourself to live more fully, integrate unconscious aspects of your personality, and make decisions guided by deeper wisdom.

Remember that dreams do not always provide clear answers but rather present symbols and metaphors that encourage reflection. Use the tools in this book to explore those metaphors and draw your own meaning. Trust in your intuition, as no one knows your inner landscape better than you.

Embrace Your Dreams

As you close this book, consider how your relationship with dreams has changed. Whether you seek to interpret each night's vision or simply appreciate the mystery of your subconscious, embrace your dreams as a valuable part of your life's journey. They are both your guide and your mirror, revealing the depths of who you are and who you are becoming.

This concludes the book on dream interpretation. The answers are within your reach, waiting to be unlocked. Keep exploring, keep dreaming, and allow your subconscious to reveal its wisdom.

Don't miss out!

Visit the website below and you can sign up to receive emails whenever Catherine J Rosser publishes a new book. There's no charge and no obligation.

https://books2read.com/r/B-A-FGQOC-KDSDF

BOOKS 2 READ

Connecting independent readers to independent writers.

Did you love *Dream Interpretation: A Journey Through the Mind's Mirror*? Then you should read *The Thistle Queen*[1] by Catherine J Rosser!

In the cursed forest of Thrysseldown, where shadows whisper and thorns grow thicker than hope, the Thistle Queen reigns. Once a guardian of the land, her heart was corrupted by forbidden love and betrayal, casting an ancient curse that turned the forest into a realm of twisted magic. Now, the forest thrives on fear, its paths shifting and dark creatures lurking in every shadow.

---

1. https://books2read.com/u/bayO1L

2. https://books2read.com/u/bayO1L

Elowen, a humble gardener with an extraordinary connection to the earth, stumbles upon a long-forgotten secret—the truth of the Thistle Queen's curse. Alongside Rook, a roguish thief with a haunted past, and Periwinkle, a cursed fae prince in the form of a fox, Elowen embarks on a perilous quest to restore the forest and free its people from the Queen's relentless grasp.

As they journey deeper into the heart of Thrysseldown, battling ancient magic and facing their darkest fears, they unravel the tragic history of the Queen and her once-sacred bond to the forest. But breaking the curse comes with a price, and not everyone will survive the trials of the forest. In a land where light and darkness blur, and sacrifice is inevitable, Elowen must decide how far she is willing to go to restore balance and confront the Queen who was once the forest's savior.

The Thistle Queen is a dark fairytale of magic, sacrifice, and redemption, set in a world where the forest holds its own secrets, and even the deepest love can turn to ruin.

Read more at https://catherinejrosser.com/.

Also by Catherine J Rosser

The Eternal Magic Series
The Magic Within

The Isles of Fate Series
The Crimson Raven: A Tale of Captain Poppie O'Malley
The Siren's Call: A Tale of Love and Treachery on the High Seas
Winds of Fortune

Standalone
Beyond the Horizon
Echoes in the Abyss
Haven Falls
The Fractured Mind
The Next Chapter: Embracing Midlife with Purpose, Peace, and
Possibility
The Thistle Queen
Dream Interpretation: A Journey Through the Mind's Mirror

Watch for more at https://catherinejrosser.com/.

About the Author

Catherine J. Rosser is a fantasy author who weaves together myth, magic, and unforgettable journeys. Known for her vivid storytelling and rich characters, she brings epic worlds to life with themes of destiny and self-discovery. When not writing, Catherine draws inspiration from nature, channeling its beauty into her imaginative tales.

Read more at https://catherinejrosser.com/.